# italian

## *perfection*

HINKLER
BOOKS

# italian *perfection*

Food Editor
**Neil Hargreaves**

HINKLER
BOOKS

First published in 2007 by Hinkler Books Pty Ltd
45–55 Fairchild Street
Heatherton, Victoria, 3202, Australia
www.hinklerbooks.com

2 4 6 8 10 9 7 5 3
08 10 12 11 09

ISBN: 978 1 7418 1472 9

Printed and bound in China

# contents

# an introduction to italian cooking

Italian cooking in the minds of some people is synonymous with pasta. It's true that pasta is very popular in Italy, but so too is rice, which grows in northern Italy. Soups are also very popular, varying from region to region and from season to season. Meats, fish, crustaceans and shell-fish with vegetables (either cooked or served as salads) make up the *secondo piatto* (second course). Fresh fruit and a variety of cheeses complete the meal, which is then finished with a cup of espresso coffee.

## eating habits

Traditionally, the main meal in Italy is lunch. With most offices, shops and schools closed between 1pm and 4pm, and with some public offices closing down for the day at 2pm, lunch in an Italian household is on the table any time after 1pm. For those who have only a one-hour break, lunch is still a very important meal. Whether at home, in the restaurant around the corner from the office, or at the *mensa* (the refectory or canteen), lunch is comprised of the *primo piatto* (first course) of soup, rice or pasta, followed by the *secondo piatto* (second course) of meat or fish, together with cheeses, vegetables or salad, and finally fruit.

The evening meal, any time after 8pm, could be a lighter version of lunch. However, the pasta is often replaced by a light soup with very small pasta-shapes cooked for only a few minutes, and a frittata might replace the meat dish. For the evening meal, the emphasis is on easily digestible foods: vegetables, salads, cheeses and fruit. Bread (but not butter) is part of every meal. Italians prefer to have a very light breakfast: a cappuccino or an espresso coffee, and perhaps a small cake from the local coffee-bar on the way to work. Caffè latte and biscuits, a thick slice of homemade cake, or bread and butter with jam, make up the more homely Italian breakfast.

## the daily bread

Bread has an almost transcendental role in Italian eating habits, and bakers are the high priests of Italian cooking habits. During the 1950s and 1960s there were attempts to replace the local *panetteria* (bread shop) with mass-produced bread, but common sense, and the Italian love for traditional bread-making, defeated the invading industrial moguls. The *panettieri* (bakers) resumed their traditional role in the lives of Italians. Today, thousands of *panettieri* prepare regional breads, differing in shape, taste, texture and ingredients, and continue the tradition that started soon after 168 BC, when Macedonian freed slaves baked bread for the Roman Empire.

The popular *pasta dura* bread, typical of Emilia-Romagna, is considered to be the oldest type of bread, going back to Egypt via Rome. The most extraordinary breads come from the two largest Italian islands – Sicily and Sardinia. Sicilian bread, with its unusual shapes and sprinkling of sesame seeds, bears the marks of the Saracen occupation, but perhaps the most unusual bread is the *carta da musica* (music paperbread) from Sardinia. Made from unleavened dough, this wafer-thin bread was originally used by Sardinian shepherds during their lengthy periods away from home. Today, however, the *carta da musica* (so-called because, when eaten, it sounds like music) has become a symbol of refined living and discerning cuisine.

## stepping back in time

The history of Italian gastronomy goes back to pre-Roman times, and consists of a long list of 'imported' and 'exported' foods. The first Romans were shepherds and farmers who soon learned how to evaporate sea water to produce salt for their sheep. When the production of salt was surplus to their needs, they started to export to Greek settlements in the south and to the Etruscans in the north. It was the beginning of a very profitable trade, as testified by the name of one of the main roads leading to Rome – the *Via Salaria* (Salt Road) – which was used by Roman salt exporters.

By the second century BC, Roman cuisine had become more complex. Herbs and spices brought back to Rome by Roman legionnaires were added to basic foods, and different sauces were developed – including the *garum* sauce (a fish-based sauce) and the *agrodolce* sauce, still in use today. These sauces were indiscriminately splashed on every dish.

The extravagant and excessive cooking and eating habits of the new-rich in the last days of the Roman Empire are depicted in the film *Satyricon*. Not until the banquets of the Renaissance was there again such incredible gastronomical extravagance.

The Crusaders introduced buckwheat to Italy, and then to Europe. They also reintroduced lemons and spices, many of which had been known to the Romans. Marco Polo did not introduce noodles to Italy, but his trip to the East eventually led to the opening up of a direct route to the spices of the Far East, and his countrymen, the Venetians, became wealthy importers and exporters of spices and coffee. With the discovery of the New World, peppers, tomatoes and potatoes (among other palatable foods) were introduced to Italy and soon became part of Italian culinary traditions. Maize, which is now used to make polenta, was accepted by Italian palates in 1650. By the end of the 17th century, Italian cooking and eating habits had reached full maturity.

Italian regional foods have migrated from their places of origin. Such was the destiny of the Neapolitan pizza, which at first crawled rather slowly to other parts of Italy, and then expanded throughout the world and is now known virtually everywhere now.

## towards the future

It took centuries to perfect the cooking habits and techniques that we now recognise as 'Italian cooking'; centuries to move from the plain, the bland and the basic to the extravagant, the astonishing and the complex. Roman soldiers and citizens of the second century BC ate a basic polenta-type dish, but by the time of the declining Roman Empire there were the extraordinary banquets of the rich and famous.

With the fall of the Roman Empire, hordes of barbarians invaded the peninsula, and cooking became plain once more, with very few herbs to enhance flavours. During the Renaissance, culinary excesses were counterbalanced by the less flamboyant meals of the wealthy Florentine merchants, and the less-rich Florentines, who had an even simpler form of cooking. In fact, apart from festivities or celebrations, the Florentines of the Renaissance generally preferred a rather uncomplicated style of cooking. In so doing they were following the advice of Platina, librarian of the Vatican. In his book *De Honesta Voluptate ac Valetudine (Concerning Honest Pleasure and Well-Being)*, Platina recommended moderation. The success of Platina's book clearly indicates the importance achieved by the art of cooking during the 15th century.

The increasing interest in gastronomy is further illustrated by the foundation of the first modern cooking academy, the *Compagnia del Paiolo* (Company of the Cauldron) in Florence. One of its most famous members was the painter Andrea del Sarto who prepared for the Compagnia – a dish representing a temple resting on a multi-coloured gelatine. Sausages and wedges of Parmesan cheese were used to represent the temple's columns. Inside the temple was a music-stand holding a book, with pages made of sheets of pasta, and the musical notes represented by grains of pepper.

It is this sort of extravagant combination of ingredients (and richness of colours) that we find again, four centuries later, in Marinetti's *Futurist Cookbook*. It is interesting to see that cooking utensils penetrated one of the most formal institutions of the 16th century: the *Accademia della Crusca* (Academy of the Bran). Founded in 1582, the academy was founded in order to establish and safeguard the correct use of the Tuscan language. One of the symbols used by the academy was, and still is, the wooden shovel used by bakers. It represents the 'sifting' of the good usage of the language from the bad!

Florence was the cradle of the Renaissance in every field, including gastronomy, and the influence of Florence on the rest of the then-known world was unchallenged. But it was not the uncomplicated and healthy cooking habits recommended by Platina that conquered French palates. It was the rich, voluptuous and sumptuous cuisine of the Florentine court that appealed to Francis I, and which his daughter-in-law (Catherine de' Medici) took back to France. A new gastronomic era was beginning for the French Court, and new horizons were opening up – with all the subtleties and variations of Italian cuisine.

Today, Italian cuisine remains one of the most popular styles of cooking around the world.

# appetisers

# focaccia bread

## ingredients

50 g dried yeast
1 teaspoon honey
¼ cup warm water
750 g plain flour
¼ cup extra virgin olive oil, plus
   1 tablespoon for brushing over the
   focaccia
½ cup black olives, pitted
handful sea salt
2 sprigs rosemary, pulled off the stalks
**serves 4**

1 Dissolve the yeast and honey in the warm water. Place the flour onto work surface and make a well in the centre. Pour the yeast mixture and the olive oil into the well. Work the flour into the wet mixture slowly; add more warm water if necessary.

**i**

**preparation time**
2 hours 15 minutes

**cooking time**
20 minutes

**nutritional value**
fat: 17 g
carbohydrate: 94 g
protein: 13.5 g

2 Once the mixture has formed into a dough, knead for around 10 minutes, until the dough is smooth and elastic. Place into a large oiled bowl and cover with a damp cloth. Let the dough rise for 2 hours.

3 Preheat the oven to 200°C.

4 Grease a large baking tray. Remove the risen dough from the bowl and punch out the dough, then place on the tray and roll out the dough to the size of the tray. Brush with the remaining olive oil. Scatter the olives over the dough and press them into the dough. Sprinkle a good handful of sea salt over the dough and lastly the rosemary. Place into the oven and bake for 15–20 minutes or until golden brown. Remove and cool before cutting.

# walnut pesto

### ingredients

2 cups walnuts, toasted
3 cloves garlic, peeled
4 handfuls fresh basil
3 handfuls fresh flat-leaf parsley
½ teaspoon white pepper
⅔ cup extra virgin olive oil
juice of 1 lemon
salt and pepper
**makes approximately 2½ cups**

i

**preparation time**
6 minutes

**cooking time**
10 minutes

**nutritional value**
fat: 54.5 g
carbohydrate: 1.5 g
protein: 6.5 g

**1** Preheat the oven to 180°C. Place walnuts on an oven tray and roast for 10 minutes, shaking the tray once after 5–6 minutes. Remove and set aside to cool.

**2** Place all ingredients except for the oil and lemon in a food processor. Pulse several times until ingredients start to combine.

**3** Turn processor on and slowly add the oil in a steady stream. Once all of the oil has been added, add the lemon juice. Adjust seasoning.

# almond and cumin pesto

## ingredients

½ cup almond meal
1 tablespoon cumin
1 tablespoon hazelnut meal
½ teaspoon sugar
1 tablespoon water
salt and white pepper to taste
150 ml extra virgin olive oil
**makes around 1 cup of pesto**

**i**

**preparation time**
3 minutes

**cooking time**
3 minutes

**nutritional value**
fat: 43 g
carbohydrate: 1 g
protein: 3 g

**1** Cook the dry almond meal in a dry frying pan until toasted and medium brown, being careful not to burn it. Set aside.

**2** Dry fry the cumin in the same pan until it's just beginning to smoke, stir immediately then remove from the heat. Continue to stir until the pan cools down.

**3** Combine the almond meal, cumin and all other ingredients except the oil in a food processor and blend. Slowly add the oil in a steady stream. Adjust seasoning if necessary.

# aioli italia

### ingredients

3 cloves garlic
salt
1 egg yolk, at room temperature
juice of half a lemon
1 cup light olive oil
white pepper
**makes around 1¼ cups**

**1** Place garlic and 1 teaspoon salt in a food processor, pulse briefly. Add the egg yolk and lemon juice, and pulse on and off until blended.

**2** Slowly add the oil in a steady stream. Add a pinch of white pepper and adjust the salt to taste.

**3** To thin out the aioli at any stage, add a small dash of room-temperature water and continue adding the remainder of the oil.

**preparation time**
3 minutes

**nutritional value**
fat: 39 g
carbohydrate:
0.5 g

# anchovy and caper dipping sauce

### ingredients

16 salted anchovies
¾ cup salted capers
2 cups extra virgin olive oil
**makes around 2¼ cups**

**preparation time**
3 minutes

**cooking time**
12 minutes

**nutritional value**
fat: 57.5 g
carbohydrate: 1.5 g
protein: 2 g

**1** Rinse the salt from the anchovies, dry them with paper towel and chop into small pieces. Wash and drain the capers, then chop them finely.

**2** In a small heavy-based frying pan, warm up olive oil. Add the anchovies and cook for 2 minutes until anchovies start to disintegrate. Add the capers and cook for a further 10 minutes. The sauce is ready once the anchovies have completely broken down and the sauce is smooth.

# herbed olive oil sabayon

## ingredients

4 leaves chervil
4 leaves tarragon
4 leaves parsley
2 cups dry white wine
½ cup white-wine vinegar
2 medium shallots, peeled and chopped
4 egg yolks
⅔ cup extra virgin olive oil
salt and freshly ground pepper
**makes around 1½ cups**

**i**

**preparation time**
4 minutes

**cooking time**
2 minutes

**nutritional value**
fat: 14g
carbohydrate: 0g
protein: 1g

**1** Pick the stems off all of the herbs, Heat a heavy-based saucepan and simmer the wine, vinegar, shallots and herb stems together over medium heat to reduce by approximately ⅓ cup in volume. Strain into a pouring jug and keep warm.

**2** Put the egg yolks in a blender and then, with the blender running, slowly pour in the warm liquid followed by the olive oil. Turn blender off.

**3** Chop and add the herb leaves and salt and pepper to taste, pulse the blender once or twice, then remove to a warm bowl. Serve warm within 1 hour.

# asparagus with pecorino and pancetta

### ingredients

500 g asparagus
juice of 1 lemon
100 ml extra virgin olive oil
sea salt
freshly ground black pepper
8 thin slices of pancetta, cut into pieces
pecorino cheese, shaved
**serves 4**

i

**preparation time**
4 minutes

**cooking time**
4 minutes

**nutritional value**
fat: 22 g
carbohydrate: 1.5 g
protein: 7 g

**1** Trim off the thick asparagus ends and cook asparagus in boiling water for 4 minutes until tender but still crisp. Run under cold water until asparagus is cool, then dry with paper towel.

**2** For the dressing, place the lemon juice in a bowl and slowly add the oil, whisking, until thick. Season with salt and pepper.

**3** Pour the dressing over asparagus, and serve with the pancetta and pecorino cheese shavings.

# black olive fontina pâté

## ingredients

8 cloves garlic
220 g fontina cheese, cut into
   small cubes
1 cup oil-cured black olives, pitted
¼ cup olive oil
1 loaf of crusty bread to serve
**serves 4**

1 Preheat the oven to 180°C. Wrap the garlic cloves in foil and bake for 30 minutes. Remove from oven, open foil and let cool slightly.

2 While the garlic cloves are cooling, melt the fontina cheese in a double-boiler over simmering water, stirring until smooth.

3 Using a food processor, blend olives, garlic and olive oil for 20 seconds. Add melted cheese and pulse for 10 more seconds until combined.

4 Spoon out into a serving dish and cover tightly with the plastic wrap, leaving no room for air at the top. Refrigerate for 30 minutes before serving.

i

**preparation time**
35 minutes

**cooking time**
30 minutes

**nutritional value**
fat: 18.5 g
carbohydrate: 6 g
protein: 10 g

# bagna cauda

### ingredients

½ cup plus 2 tablespoons extra virgin
  olive oil
4 cloves garlic, crushed
8 anchovies in olive oil, drained and
  chopped
½ cup unsalted butter, cut into cubes
*for dipping*
raw vegetables, such as; cauliflower,
  endive, fennel, capsicum, zucchini
  sliced into bite-sized fingers
**serves 4**

**i**

**preparation time**
6 minutes

**cooking time**
3 minutes

**nutritional value**
fat: 64 g
carbohydrate: 5 g
protein: 6 g

**1** Put the olive oil in a heavy-based saucepan with the garlic and anchovies and cook on a low heat, stirring, until the anchovies and oil have combined.

**2** Whisk in the butter, remove from the heat immediately and continue to whisk for 1 minute until combined.

**3** Pour into a warmed dish to serve. If you can, place the sauce above a tea candle (a fondue set is perfect) to keep warm while you dip in the raw vegetables.

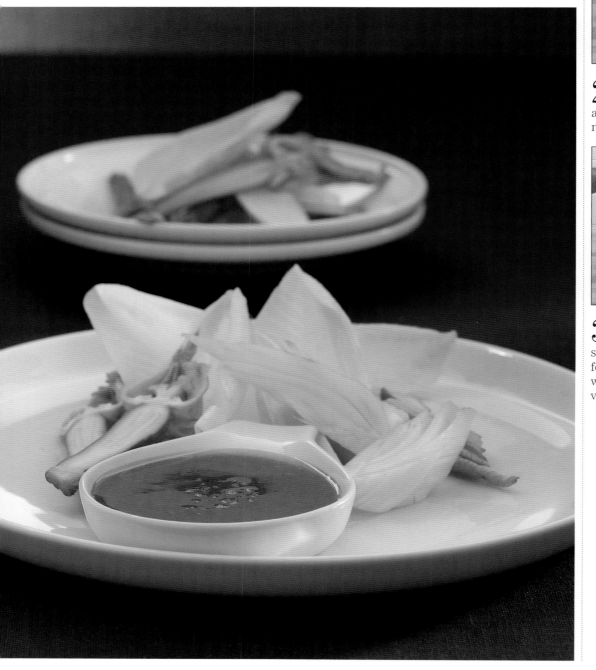

# bruschetta with bocconcini and basil

### ingredients

1 ciabatta loaf
¼ cup olive oil
⅓ cup sun-dried tomato paste
180 g bocconcini cheese, each ball
  sliced into 5
½ cup basil leaves, shredded or whole
**serves 4**

**preparation time**
4 minutes

**cooking time**
3 minutes

**nutritional value**
fat: 21.5 g
carbohydrate: 34 g
protein: 13 g

**1** Slice the bread into 2 cm thick slices.

**2** Grill ciabatta slices on each side for 2–3 minutes.

**3** Brush ciabatta with olive oil, spread with sun-dried tomato paste, and top with bocconcini slices and basil.

# mozzarella with garlic and caper berries

### ingredients

500 g fresh mozzarella cheese
*dressing*
2 cloves garlic, chopped
4 tablespoons olive oil
2 tablespoons balsamic vinegar
1 tablespoon fresh oregano, chopped
1 teaspoon salt
½ teaspoon ground black pepper
*garnish*
caper berries
black olives
fresh oregano
**serves 4**

**i**

**preparation time**
10 minutes

**nutritional value**
fat: 18.5 g
carbohydrate: 3.5 g
protein: 0.5 g

**1** Slice the mozzarella into 1 cm slices. Place slices on to a serving dish.

**2** Place the dressing ingredients in a bowl and stir to combine. Pour the dressing over the sliced mozzarella.

**3** Garnish with the caper berries, olives and oregano.

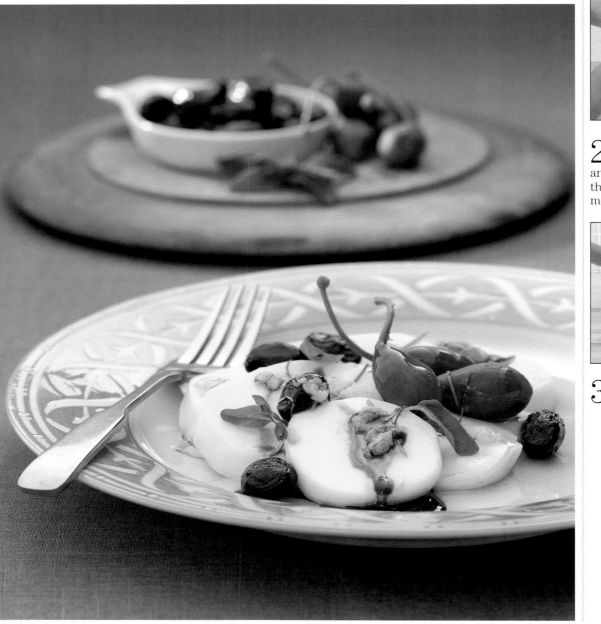

# olive and lemon potatoes

## ingredients

650 g potatoes, peeled
8 to 10 garlic cloves
2 teaspoons salt
2 egg yolks
freshly ground black pepper
½ to 1 cup extra virgin olive oil
juice of 1 lemon

**serves 4 as a side dish**

1 Preheat the oven to 220°C. Bake the potatoes for approximately 30 minutes, then let cool slightly.

2 Meanwhile, process the garlic and salt in a food processor until smooth, add the egg yolks and pulse briefly to combine.

3 Break each potato in half, and put one half at a time in a potato ricer, and press it through into a bowl. Continue until all of the potatoes have been riced. Use a rubber spatula to fold the garlic mixture into the riced potatoes. Add the pepper and mix in the olive oil 1 tablespoon at a time, until the mixture is thick and dense and will not absorb any more oil.

4 Add the lemon juice.

**preparation time**
10 minutes

**cooking time**
30 minutes

**nutritional value**
fat: 30 g
carbohydrate: 15 g
protein: 4 g

# roasted garlic polenta

## ingredients

2 bulbs garlic
1 shallot, finely diced
1 teaspoon salt
1½ L water
250 g fast cooking polenta
50 g butter
50 g parmesan cheese, grated
¼ bunch basil, chopped

**serves 4**

*i*

**preparation time**
3 minutes

**cooking time**
52 minutes

**nutritional value**
fat: 10.5 g
carbohydrate: 29 g
protein: 7 g

**1** Preheat the oven to 200°C. Wrap the garlic in foil and roast for 45 minutes to 1 hour. Remove from the oven and squeeze out the garlic from the skins.

**2** Place the shallot, salt and water into a saucepan and bring to the boil. Pour the polenta into the boiling water and stir continuously for 5 minutes.

**3** Stir the garlic through the polenta. Stir through butter and parmesan. Cook for 2 minutes. Serve topped with basil accompanied by chargrilled vegetables.

# chargrilled vegetables with pesto

## ingredients

1 capsicum
1 eggplant
2 zucchinis
2 red onions
1 small sweet potato
olive oil
**serves 4**

**i**

**preparation time**
5 minutes

**cooking time**
10 minutes

**nutritional value**
fat: 0.5 g
carbohydrate: 13 g
protein: 3.5 g

1 Slice capsicum and zucchini lengthways into long pieces.

2 Slice eggplant and sweet potato diagonally and cut onions into 4 large pieces.

3 Grease and heat a chargrill pan. Brush vegetable slices with a little olive oil and chargrill until vegetables are cooked and golden brown.

4 Arrange vegetables in layers on a large serving platter or in a small mound on each plate. Serve with walnut pesto (see recipe page 11).

# soups, pasta and rice

# roasted tomato, red capsicum and bread soup

### ingredients

1 kg roma tomatoes
2 red capsicums, roughly chopped
40 ml olive oil
3 cloves garlic, crushed
2 onions, finely chopped
2 teaspoons cumin
1 teaspoon ground coriander
1 L chicken stock
2 slices white bread, crusts removed
  and torn into pieces
20 ml balsamic vinegar
salt and freshly ground pepper to taste
parmesan cheese, grated

**serves 4**

i

**preparation time**
10  minutes

**cooking time**
1 hour

**nutritional value**
fat: 13 g
carbohydrate: 17 g
protein: 10.5 g

**1** Preheat the oven to 220°C and cut tomatoes.

**2** Place tomatoes and capsicums in a lightly oiled baking dish and bake for 20 minutes, or until the skins have blistered. Set aside to cool, then remove skins and roughly chop.

**3** Heat the oil in a saucepan, add the garlic and the onion, and cook for 5 minutes or until soft. Add cumin and coriander and cook for 1 minute. Add tomatoes, capsicums and stock to the saucepan, bring to the boil, and simmer for 30 minutes. Add bread, balsamic vinegar, salt and pepper, and cook a further 5–10 minutes.

**4** Serve with parmesan cheese, if desired.

# sweet potato and rosemary soup

### ingredients

40 ml olive oil
2 cloves garlic, crushed
1 medium onion, chopped
1 tablespoon rosemary, chopped
2 tablespoons tomato paste
1 medium carrot, diced
1 large potato, diced
750 g sweet potato, diced
1 L chicken stock
salt and freshly ground pepper
2 tablespoons rosemary, chopped, extra

**serves 4-6**

**1** Heat oil in a saucepan, add the garlic, onion and rosemary, and cook on medium heat for 3–5 minutes or until soft.

**2** Add the tomato pesto and cook for 1 minute.

**3** Add carrot, potato and sweet potato, and cook a further 5 minutes. Add the chicken stock, salt and pepper, bring to boil, reduce the heat and simmer with the lid on for 30–40 minutes, or until vegetables are soft.

**4** Purée the soup in a food processor (you may have to do this in two batches). Return the soup to pan, add the rosemary and heat through before serving. Add extra stock if soup is too thick.

---

**i**

**preparation time**
10 minutes

**cooking time**
50 minutes

**nutritional value**
fat: 11.5 g
carbohydrate: 28 g
protein: 7 g

# jerusalem artichoke soup

## ingredients

50 g butter
6 slices pancetta
1 large onion, peeled and thinly sliced
1 leek, thinly sliced then soaked and washed
1 stalk celery, peeled and thinly sliced
2 cloves garlic, peeled
salt and freshly ground white pepper
bouquet garni
1 kg jerusalem artichokes, cleaned and cut into thick slices
1 small potato, peeled and diced
2 L unsalted chicken stock
¾ cup extra virgin olive oil

**serves 4**

**i**

**preparation time**
35 minutes

**cooking time**
1 hour 10 minutes

**nutritional value**
fat: 12 g
carbohydrate: 4 g
protein: 3.5 g

**1** Melt the butter in a large saucepan over medium heat. Add the pancetta and cook for 5 minutes, stirring occasionally. Add the onion, leek, celery, garlic and the bouquet garni, cook for 5 minutes, stirring occasionally. Add the artichokes and the potato and cook for 15 to 20 minutes, stirring occasionally.

**2** Add the stock and bring the mixture to the boil. Lower the heat to a simmer and cook, uncovered, for 35 minutes. Discard the bouquet garni.

**3** Working in batches, purée the soup in a food processor and add the salt and pepper to taste. Add the olive oil to the soup and bring to the simmer.

# garlic soup

## ingredients

2 tablespoons olive oil
2 tablespoons butter
1 kg onions, sliced
2 cups cloves garlic, chopped
6 stems parsley
8 sprigs fresh thyme
1 bay leaf
2 cups milk
2 L chicken stock
2 large potatoes, peeled and diced
1½ teaspoons salt
½ teaspoon ground pepper
extra parsley, to garnish
parmesan cheese, to garnish

**serves 4–6**

**i**

**preparation time**
10 minutes

**cooking time**
1 hour

**nutritional value**
fat: 21 g
carbohydrate: 33 g
protein: 16 g

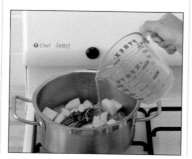

**1** In a large saucepan, heat the olive oil and butter. Add the onions and garlic, and cook on a medium heat stirring frequently until very soft: about 30 minutes. Tie the parsley stems, thyme and bay leaf together with kitchen string.

**2** Add the chicken stock, potatoes and salt to the onions. Add to the pot. Bring to the boil, reduce the heat and simmer for 15 minutes. Remove from the heat and take out the herbs.

**3** Purée in a food processor. Strain the pureed soup back into the saucepan. Add the milk and pepper, place back on to the heat and bring back to the boil.

**4** Garnish with fresh parsley and parmesan.

# garlic and bean soup

## ingredients

200 g pancetta
8 cloves garlic
1 tablespoon butter
1 onion finely diced
2 stalks celery, diced
2 L chicken stock
3 roma tomatoes, peeled, seeded and diced
2 zucchinis, diced
2 tablespoons fresh thyme
2 bay leaves
425 g can cannellini beans
425 g can borlotti beans
salt and freshly ground pepper

**serves 4**

i

**preparation time**
15 minutes

**cooking time**
40 minutes

**nutritional value**
fat: 14.5 g
carbohydrate: 53 g
protein: 36 g

1 Dice the pancetta. Slice the garlic.

2 Melt butter in a large saucepan. Add the onion and garlic and cook until transparent. Add the pancetta and cook for 3 minutes. Add the celery and cook for a further 2 minutes. Add the stock, tomatoes, zucchini, thyme and bay leaves. Cook for 15 minutes.

3 Add the beans and cook for a further 20 mins. Season the soup with salt and freshly ground black pepper. Serve in bowls.

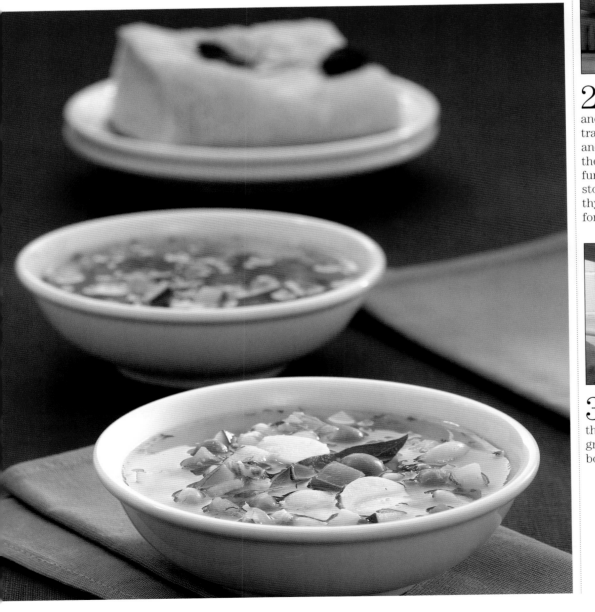

# spaghetti with garlic and anchovies

## ingredients

500 g spaghetti
6 cloves garlic
4 tablespoons olive oil, plus extra
  to serve
1 tablespoon butter
8 anchovies, roughly chopped
½ small bunch of flat-leaf parsley,
  finely chopped
salt and freshly ground pepper
parmesan cheese, shaved

**serves 4**

**1** Cook spaghetti according to packet directions.

i

**preparation time**
8 minutes

**cooking time**
10 minutes

**nutritional value**
fat: 24.5 g
carbohydrate: 86 g
protein: 16.5 g

**2** Meanwhile peel the garlic, add a pinch of salt and crush with the flat of a knife to make a fine paste. Heat olive oil and butter in a pan. Add the garlic to the pan and cook for 1 minute. Add the anchovies and cook until they melt into the garlic: approximately 2 minutes.

**3** Add the spaghetti and parsley to the garlic and anchovy mix and toss to combine. Season to taste.

**4** Top with shaved parmesan and a drizzle of olive oil.

# smoked salmon ravioli with lemon dill sauce

## ingredients

125 g smoked salmon pieces
1 egg white
1½ tablespoons cream
2 teaspoons fresh dill, roughly chopped
2–3 tablespoons cornflour
32 wonton skins
1 teaspoon oil
*lemon dill sauce*
1 tablespoon butter
1 tablespoon flour
¾ cup white wine
¾ cup thickened cream
juice of half a lemon
2 tablespoons dill, roughly chopped
salt and freshly ground black pepper
**serves 4**

i

**preparation time**
20 minutes

**cooking time**
15 minutes

**nutritional value**
fat: 30 g
carbohydrate: 13 g
protein: 10 g

1 Place the salmon, 1 tablespoon of egg white, cream and dill in a food processor, and process until well combined, like a mousse.

2 Sprinkle the cornflour on a work surface and lay wonton skins in rows of four.

3 Brush every second skin around the edge with egg white. On alternate skins, place a teaspoon of mixture in the middle. Place the other skins on top and gently pinch around the mixture, so they look like pillows or rounds.

4 Half fill a large saucepan with water and oil, bring to the boil and add 2–3 cups ravioli. Cook for 2–3 minutes. Set aside and cover with plastic wrap.

5 To make the lemon dill sauce, melt the butter in a saucepan, add the flour and cook for 1 minute. Add the wine and then stir until smooth, add the cream and lemon juice. Bring to the boil and reduce until sauce has a pouring consistency.

6 To serve, add the dill, salt and pepper to the sauce and pour over ravioli.

# pæsani pasta with rocket and spicy pancetta

**ingredients**

500 g fusilli pæsani
1 tablespoon extra virgin olive oil
2 cloves garlic, crushed
100g hot pancetta, roughly chopped
1 cup tomato pasta sauce
100 g semi-sun-dried tomatoes
1 bunch rocket, washed and drained
salt and freshly ground black pepper
parmesan cheese, shaved
**serves 4**

1 Cook pasta in boiling salted water until al dente. Drain and set aside.

2 Heat oil in a saucepan, add garlic and pancetta and cook for 2 minutes or until garlic is soft and flavours are well combined.

3 Add the pasta, tomato sauce, semi-sun-dried tomatoes, rocket, salt and pepper to the pan, and heat through.

4 Serve with parmesan cheese.

i

**preparation time**
3 minutes

**cooking time**
15 minutes

**nutritional value**
fat: 13 g
carbohydrate: 101 g
protein: 25.5 g

# linguine with prawns, zucchini flowers and olive oil sauce

### ingredients

800 g linguine
12 zucchini flowers
3 cloves garlic, crushed
½ cup extra virgin olive oil
1 large onion, diced
12 prawns, shells and heads removed
1 tablespoons thyme, chopped
juice of 1 lemon
salt and freshly ground black pepper
**serves 4**

**i**

**preparation time**
12 minutes

**cooking time**
10 minutes

**nutritional value**
fat: 31.5 g
carbohydrate: 157 g
protein: 38 g

**1** Boil water for pasta in a saucepan and add the linguine.

**2** Cut the flowers off the zucchini. Slice the baby zucchini into rounds and coat with the crushed garlic and some of the olive oil.

**3** Slice zucchini flowers into quarters.

**4** Sweat the onion in the remaining olive oil, add prawns and zucchini and fry slowly until just cooked.

**5** When pasta is al dente, drain and combine with the thyme, zucchini flowers, lemon juice and season with salt and pepper.

# umbrian chilli garlic spaghetti

### ingredients

500 g spaghetti
½ cup extra virgin olive oil
1 clove garlic, thinly sliced
1½ tablespoons green chilli, freshly chopped and deseeded
1 teaspoon fresh ginger, chopped
1 teaspoon salt
1 teaspoon freshly ground black pepper
½ cup fresh Italian flat-leaf parsley, finely chopped
1 tablespoon lemon juice
**serves 4**

**i**

**preparation time**
8 minutes

**cooking time**
12 minutes

**nutritional value**
fat: 44g
carbohydrate: 86g
protein: 14g

1 Boil water in saucepan and add the spaghetti.

2 In a heavy-based frying pan, heat the oil, then add garlic, chilli, ginger, salt and pepper and cook until garlic starts to turn golden in colour.

3 Add the parsley and lemon juice, reduce heat and keep warm until pasta is cooked.

4 When pasta is al dente, strain, add to the pan of sauce and toss to combine.

# garlic and copocollo risotto

### ingredients

1 blub garlic, roasted
250 g broad beans
14 thin slices copocollo
1 tablespoon olive oil
1 small onion, finely diced
2 cups arborio rice
2 tablespoons white wine
6 cups chicken stock
25 g butter
½ cup parmesan cheese, grated

**serves 4**

1 Preheat the oven to 200°C. Wrap the garlic bulb tightly in foil and roast in the oven for 50 minutes.

2 Scald the broad beans in boiling water, then quickly plunge in ice-cold water and drain. Remove the beans from their skins.

3 Dice 8 slices of the copocollo. Squeeze the garlic out of the skin and set aside.

4 Heat a heavy-based saucepan. Add the olive oil and fry the onion and copocollo for 3 minutes, stirring constantly. Add the rice and continue to stir for another 3 minutes. Add the roasted garlic and the white wine, then add the stock one cup at a time, stirring constantly. Continue until all the stock is absorbed: approximately 20 minutes.

5 Stir through the butter, parmesan and broad beans and cook for 2 more minutes. Season to taste and garnish with the remaining copocollo slices.

**i**

**preparation time**
15 minutes

**cooking time**
1 hour 15 minutes

**nutritional value**
fat: 19.5 g
carbohydrate: 90 g
protein: 26.5 g

# poultry
# and meat

# butterflied quail with lemon and sage leaves

### ingredients

40 ml olive oil
20 ml lemon juice
½ teaspoon lemon zest
1 clove garlic, crushed
freshly ground pepper
sea salt
1 tablespoon olive oil, extra
4 quails, butterflied
1 bunch sage leaves: 1 tablespoon
  chopped, the rest for garnish
¼ cup chicken stock

**serves 4**

**1** Preheat the oven to 180°C.

**2** Combine the olive oil, lemon juice, lemon zest, garlic, pepper and salt in a bowl. Set aside.

**3** Heat the extra oil in a large frying pan, add the quail and the chopped sage leaves, and brown quickly. Set aside.

**4** To the pan, add the lemon juice mixture and the chicken stock. Return to the heat, bring to the boil and simmer for 1 minute to reduce, stirring with a wooden spoon.

**5** Pour the sauce over the quail, transfer to an ovenproof dish and bake in the oven for 20–25 minutes. Garnish with whole sage leaves.

**i**

**preparation time**
10 minutes

**cooking time**
30 minutes

**nutritional value**
fat: 21 g
carbohydrate: 0.5 g
protein: 21 g

# chicken with basil cream sauce

### ingredients

3 tablespoons flour
salt and freshly ground black pepper
4 chicken breasts
1 tablespoon olive oil
1 tablespoon butter
**basil cream sauce**
1 tablespoon butter
2 cloves garlic, crushed
½ cup chicken stock
½ cup cream
¼ cup lemon juice
2 tablespoons basil, finely chopped
freshly ground pepper
sea salt
**serves 4**

1 Combine the flour, pepper and salt in a bowl and coat the chicken evenly with the mixture, shaking off the excess.

2 Heat the oil and butter in a pan, add the chicken and cook over medium heat for 5–6 minutes each side. Remove from the pan and keep warm.

3 To make the basil cream sauce, wipe out the pan, heat the butter, add the garlic and cook for 2 minutes. Add the chicken stock, cream and lemon juice, bring to the boil and reduce a little.

4 Just before serving, add the basil, season with pepper and salt and pour the sauce over the chicken.

i

**preparation time**
5 minutes

**cooking time**
15 minutes

**nutritional value**
fat: 42 g
carbohydrate: 8 g
protein: 63.5 g

# chicken saltimbocca

## ingredients

4 small chicken breasts
2-3 tablespoons butter
220 g mozzarella, sliced into 8 rounds
8 slices prosciutto
12 sage leaves

### sauce

2 teaspoons sage, roughly chopped
½ cup white wine
¼ cup chicken stock

**serves 4**

**i**

**preparation time**
12 minutes

**cooking time**
6 minutes

**nutritional value**
fat: 34 g
carbohydrate: 0.5 g
protein: 59 g

1 Using a meat mallet, pound the chicken until thin.

2 Heat the butter in a pan, add the chicken and brown quickly on both sides. Remove from the pan and top each breast with 2 slices mozzarella, 2 slices prosciutto and 2–3 sage leaves. Secure with toothpicks.

3 Under a hot grill, cook chicken for approximately 2 minutes, until cheese has just started to melt. Set aside.

4 To make the sauce, reheat the butter, add the sage and cook for 1 minute. Add the white wine and stock and reduce the sauce slightly.

5 Pour the sauce over the chicken, and serve immediately.

# roasted garlic spatchcock

## ingredients

2 spatchcocks
3 cloves garlic, finely crushed
¼ cup extra virgin olive oil
2 tablespoons lemon juice
3 sprigs rosemary
½ teaspoon freshly ground black
    pepper
zest of 1 lemon
**serves 4**

**1** Preheat the oven to 180°C.

**2** Combine all ingredients together in a bowl, except the spatchcocks. Place the spatchcocks into a large ovenproof dish and pour over the marinade. Refrigerate for 2 hours.

**3** Roast for 30 minutes, basting the spatchcocks every 10 minutes with the marinade. To test whether the spatchcock is cooked, pierce with a sharp knife – the juices should run clear. Serve with vegetables.

**i**

**preparation time**
2 hours

**cooking time**
30 minutes

**nutritional value**
fat: 62.5 g
carbohydrate: 0.5 g
protein: 74 g

# rack of veal with thyme on roasted garlic mash

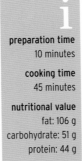

## ingredients

*mash*
1 bulb garlic
750 g potatoes, peeled and chopped
½ cup olive oil
1 tablespoon capers
salt
freshly ground black pepper
*lamb*
2 tablespoons olive oil
1 kg (8 points) rack of veal
2 tablespoons thyme leaves, chopped
300 ml white wine
300 ml chicken stock
**serves 4**

**i**

**preparation time**
10 minutes
**cooking time**
45 minutes
**nutritional value**
fat: 106 g
carbohydrate: 51 g
protein: 44 g

**1** Preheat the oven to 200°C. Wrap the garlic in foil and roast for 45 minutes to an hour. Remove from the oven and squeeze the garlic out of the skin.

**2** Boil the potatoes until soft. Drain, then mash or purée and add the olive oil, chopped capers and 1 tablespoon roasted garlic purée. Mix well, season with salt and pepper to taste and set aside.

**3** Heat olive oil in a pan and brown the veal on both sides until well sealed – approximately 5 minutes. Remove from the pan and place on a rack in a baking dish.

**4** Rub the veal with 1 tablespoon of roasted garlic purée and 1 tablespoon of thyme leaves, season with salt and pepper, and add half the wine and stock to the baking dish.

**5** Roast in the oven for 20 minutes, or until the veal is cooked to your liking. Wrap in foil and let rest for 10 minutes.

**6** Add remaining stock, wine and thyme to the pan juices and cook over a medium heat for 5 minutes, until the liquid has reduced by a third.

**7** Serve veal with mashed potatoes and the pan juices.

# lamb cutlets with olives and rosemary

### ingredients

1 tablespoon olive oil
2 cloves garlic, chopped
8-12 lamb cutlets, depending on size
²⁄₃ cup white wine
2 tablespoons tomato paste
²⁄₃ cup beef stock
2 sprigs rosemary, roughly chopped
¹⁄₃ cup black olives
freshly ground black pepper
**serves 4**

1 Preheat the oven to 170°C. Heat the oil in a large pan, add the garlic and lamb cutlets and brown on medium heat for 2–3 minutes on each side.

2 Add the wine and cook for 2 minutes. Mix the tomato paste with the beef stock and add to the pan, with the rosemary, black olives and pepper to taste.

3 Transfer to a casserole dish and bake for 30–40 minutes or until the lamb is cooked to your liking.

**i**

**preparation time**
2 minutes

**cooking time**
1 hour

**nutritional value**
fat: 14.5 g
carbohydrate: 4.5 g
protein: 24.5 g

# seafood
# and
# salads

# salmon cutlets with dill hollandaise sauce

## ingredients

40 ml extra virgin olive oil, plus extra
    for grilling
1 tablespoon lemon juice
2/3 teaspoon coarse black pepper
4 salmon cutlets, each 220-250 g
1 bunch asparagus

*dill hollandaise sauce*
85 ml white-wine vinegar
freshly ground black pepper
1/4 cup water
4 egg yolks
220 g unsalted butter, melted
40 ml lemon juice
3 tablespoons fresh dill, chopped

**serves 4**

1 Combine oil, lemon juice and pepper in a large ceramic dish. Add salmon cutlets and leave to marinate for 3 hours.

2 To make the sauce, put vinegar, pepper and water in a small saucepan. Bring to the boil, then reduce until 1 tablespoon of the liquid is left.

3 Place egg yolks and vinegar mixture in a food processor and process for 1 minute. With the processor still running, gradually add the hot melted butter and blend until thick.

4 Add lemon juice, dill and salt and pepper to taste, and keep warm.

5 Heat a lightly oiled chargrill pan, or preheat a grill. Cook salmon cutlets for 2–3 minutes each side, or until done to your liking.

6 Trim the asparagus and blanch it in a bowl of boiling water for 2–3 minutes.

7 Serve fish with hollandaise sauce and asparagus on the side.

i
**preparation time**
3 hours 10 minutes

**cooking time**
20 minutes

**nutritional value**
fat: 80.5 g
carbohydrate: 1.5 g
protein: 47 g

# blue-eyed cod with aioli and parmesan potatoes

### ingredients

1 clove garlic, chopped
2 tablespoons olive oil
1 tablespoon lemon juice
4 blue-eyed cod cutlets
1 quantity aioli  (see recipe page 13)
handful of basil leaves

*parmesan potatoes*

400 g potatoes, peeled and cubed
1 tablespoon olive oil
1 tablespoon butter
1 tablespoon parmesan cheese, grated

**serves 4**

*i*

**preparation time**
1 hour

**cooking time**
26 minutes

**nutritional value**
fat: 19.5 g
carbohydrate: 14 g
protein: 31 g

**1** Combine the garlic, olive oil and lemon juice in a dish, and marinate the fish cutlets for 1 hour.

**2** Grease a grill or frying pan and cook fish for 3 minutes on each side.

**3** To make the parmesan potatoes, place them in a saucepan with salted water and boil until potatoes are almost cooked, but still a little hard in the centre. Drain.

**4** Heat the oil and butter in a pan, add the potatoes and cook until brown. Add the cheese and cook until potatoes are crisp.

**5** Add basil leaves to the aioli when adding the garlic and serve the fish with the aioli and parmesan potatoes.

# garlic and lemon mussels

### ingredients

2 tablespoons olive oil
1 kg mussels
6 cloves garlic, finely chopped
1 chilli, sliced
½ bunch basil leaves, roughly chopped
4 roma tomatoes, diced
1 cup white wine
1 teaspoon salt
freshly ground black pepper
1 lemon, cut into wedges

**serves 4**

**1** Heat the oil in a heavy-based saucepan until almost smoking. Add the mussels. They should make a popping sound when they hit the oil. Cook for 1 minute.

**2** Add the garlic, chilli, basil, tomatoes and white wine. Cover with a lid and cook for a further 4 minutes.

**3** Discard any mussels that do not open during cooking. Season with salt and pepper. Serve with lemon wedges.

**i**

**preparation time**
10 minutes

**cooking time**
5 minutes

**nutritional value**
fat: 14 g
carbohydrate: 16 g
protein: 13.5 g

# calamari in garlic and capers

## ingredients

4 calamari tubes
*poaching liquid*
1 small carrot, peeled and chopped
1 small onion, peeled and chopped
½ bunch thyme
8 cloves garlic
750 ml water
juice and zest of 1 lemon
500 g capers
*marinade*
1 teaspoon cumin
100 ml extra virgin olive oil
juice of 1 lemon
½ teaspoon salt
½ teaspoon ground black pepper
8 sprigs lemon thyme
*salad*
2 small heads radicchio
1 witlof
2 teaspoon capers
½ cup flat-leaf parsley, chopped
**serves 4**

**1** Place all the ingredients for the poaching liquid in a saucepan, bring to the boil and simmer for 10 minutes.

**2** Meanwhile, clean the calamari tubes under running water. Place into the simmering poaching liquid for around 2 minutes. Remove the garlic cloves from the poaching liquid and slice. Remove the calamari from the poaching liquid and cut into 5 cm wide strips.

**3** Place the ingredients for the marinade in a bowl, add the sliced garlic and mix together. Add the sliced calamari to the marinade and refrigerate for 30 minutes.

**4** Wash the radicchio and witlof and discard the outer leaves. Place in a bowl with the capers and chopped parsley. Remove the calamari from the marinade, add it to the salad and use ½ cup of the marinade as a dressing.

**i**

**preparation time**
20 minutes

**cooking time**
12 minutes

**nutritional value**
fat: 32 g
carbohydrate: 1.5 g
protein: 17 g

# spinach, pine nut and avocado salad

## ingredients

80 g coppa ham, sliced
220 g baby spinach
60 g pine nuts, toasted
1 avocado, sliced
¼ cup olive oil
2 tablespoons balsamic vinegar
¼ cup pecorino cheese shavings
sea salt
freshly ground black pepper
**serves 4-6**

**i**

**preparation time**
5 minutes

**cooking time**
2 minutes

**nutritional value**
fat: 33.5 g
carbohydrate: 1 g
protein: 8 g

1 Place the slices of coppa under a hot grill and cook until crispy. Place spinach, coppa, pine nuts and avocado in a bowl.

2 Mix together the oil and balsamic vinegar, pour the dressing over the salad, and then toss through the pecorino shavings.

3 Season with salt and pepper and serve.

# tomato, bocconcini and basil salad

### ingredients

410 g roma tomatoes, thickly sliced
250 g bocconcini cheese, sliced
½ cup fresh basil leaves, shredded
extra virgin olive oil
balsamic vinegar
sea salt and freshly ground black
  pepper
crusty bread, for serving
**serves 4-6**

**preparation time**
10 minutes

**nutritional value**
fat: 10 g
carbohydrate:
1.5 g

1 Arrange tomatoes, bocconcini and basil leaves on individual plates.

2 Drizzle with extra virgin olive oil and balsamic vinegar, and sprinkle with sea salt and freshly ground black pepper.

3 Serve with crusty bread.

# fennel, olive and blood orange salad

## ingredients

3 small bulbs fennel
juice of 1 lemon
salt and pepper
juice of 1 orange
¼ cup extra virgin olive oil
80 g mixed salad leaves
2 oranges, segmented
⅓ cup black olives
1 cup flat-leaf parsley
100 g parmesan cheese, shaved

**serves 6**

i

**preparation time**
5 minutes

**nutritional value**
fat: 19.5 g
carbohydrate: 11 g
protein: 9.5 g

**1** Trim the tops from the fennel. Cut the bulbs in half lengthwise, then slice thinly. Toss in a stainless steel bowl with the lemon juice and seasoning.

**2** In a small bowl, whisk together the orange juice and olive oil. Combine the fennel, salad leaves, orange segments, olives and parsley. Coat with the vinaigrette and toss lightly. Serve topped with shavings of parmesan cheese.

# tuscan white beans

## ingredients

2 cloves garlic, peeled and sliced
1 cup extra virgin olive oil
1 red chilli, sliced lengthwise
5 sage leaves, finely sliced
zest and juice of 1 lemon
440 g cannellini beans, drained
  and rinsed
⅓ cup parsley, chopped
salt and white pepper
1 onion, finely diced
1 stalk celery, finely sliced
1 carrot, peeled and finely diced
**serves 4**

1 In a medium-sized heavy-based saucepan, slowly cook the garlic in half of the oil on a moderate heat. Add the chilli, half of the sage and half of the lemon juice and simmer very slowly for 15 minutes. Remove the chilli and add 2 tablespoons of cannellini beans and mash them through the oil.

**i**

**preparation time**
25 minutes

**cooking time**
15 minutes

**nutritional value**
fat: 57.5 g
carbohydrate: 19 g
protein: 10 g

2 Add ⅓ cup of chopped parsley, season to taste, stir and remove from the heat.

3 Combine the remaining ingredients, pour over the dressing and season to taste.

4 Stand for a further 15 minutes before serving.

# desserts

# passionfruit zabaglione with fresh berries

### ingredients

5 egg yolks
½ cup caster sugar
½ cup sweet white wine
85 ml passionfruit pulp
125 g blueberries
150 g raspberries
150 g strawberries

**serves 4-6**

i

**preparation time**
10 minutes

**cooking time**
15 minutes

**nutritional value**
fat: 5 g
carbohydrate: 28 g
protein: 4 g

1 Combine egg yolks and sugar in a heatproof bowl and beat until thick and pale. Beat through the sweet wine, and place the bowl over a saucepan of simmering water. Continue to beat for 15 minutes or until the mixture is very thick, not allowing the bowl to heat too much. The mixture is ready when it forms soft mounds.

2 Remove the bowl from the heat and continue beating for a further 5 minutes, or until the mixture has cooled. Fold through the passionfruit pulp and serve with the fresh berries.

# frangelico chocolate cake

## ingredients

100 g dark chocolate, chopped
50 g butter
3 eggs, separated
¼ cup caster sugar
2 tablespoons self-raising flour, sifted
¼ cup ground hazelnuts
25 ml frangelico liqueur
*sauce*
180 g raspberries
2 tablespoons icing sugar
1 tablespoon lemon juice
**serves 4**

**i**

**preparation time**
5 minutes

**cooking time**
45 minutes

**nutritional value**
fat: 25 g
carbohydrate: 40 g
protein: 7.5 g

1 Preheat the oven to 190°C. Melt the chocolate and butter over hot water, remove from the heat and stir in egg yolks, sugar, flour, hazelnuts and frangelico.

2 Beat the egg whites until soft peaks form. Fold lightly into the chocolate mixture and pour into a greased and lined 12 cm round baking tin and bake for 35–40 minutes, or until cake shrinks slightly from sides of tin.

3 To make the raspberry sauce, place raspberries, icing sugar and lemon juice in a food processor and blend until smooth. Strain, and add a little water if the mixture is too thick.

4 Serve cake cut into wedges, with raspberry sauce and cream.

# lemon and olive oil semifreddo

## ingredients

6 egg yolks
¾ cup sugar
½ cup olive oil
3 cups milk
1 cup double cream
juice of 1 lemon
40 ml limoncello liqueur
figs and honey to serve
**serves 4**

i

**preparation time**
3 hours

**cooking time**
5 minutes

**nutritional value**
fat: 30 g
carbohydrate: 22 g
protein: 4.5 g

1 Beat the egg yolks and sugar until light in colour and thick in consistency. Slowly blend in olive oil until combined.

2 Combine the milk and cream in a large heavy-based saucepan. Bring to a medium heat, until the mixture starts to simmer. Add a cup of hot milk to the eggs, whisking thoroughly, and repeat with remaining milk.

3 Return the mixture to the saucepan and stir quickly over heat for 3 minutes. When the custard starts to thicken, remove from the heat and strain through a fine mesh strainer. Add the lemon juice and the limoncello. Cool to room temperature. Pour into a tray and freeze until solid.

4 Leave out of freezer for 10 minutes, slice into pieces and serve with fresh figs and honey.

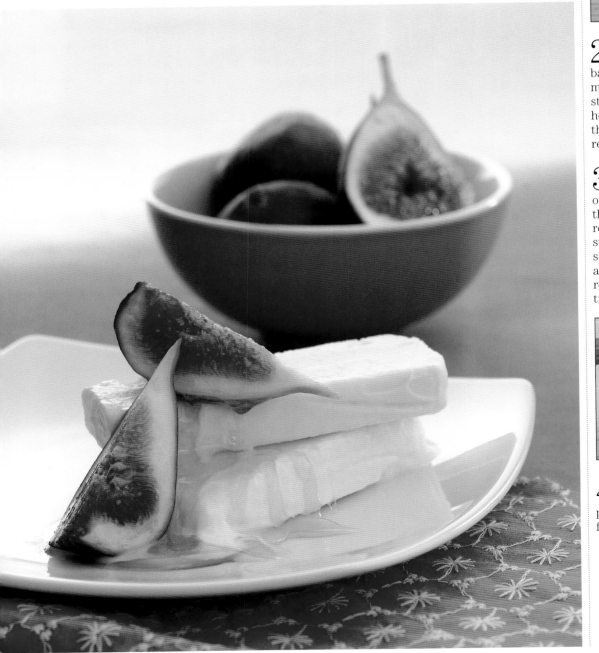

# lemon crema crunch

## ingredients

6 egg yolks
1 whole egg
600 ml double cream
3 drops vanilla extract
1 sprig rosemary
½ cup caster sugar
zest of 3 lemons
½ cup extra virgin olive oil
ice

**serves 4**

1 Preheat the oven to 160°C. Remove eggs from refrigerator. In a pot combine cream, vanilla, rosemary, sugar, lemon zest and olive oil and bring to a simmer. Do not boil or the cream will split. Remove from the heat, leave for 5 minutes, then remove the rosemary.

2 Whisk room-temperature eggs in a separate bowl.

**i**

**preparation time**
10 minutes

**cooking time**
50 minutes

**nutritional value**
fat: 115 g
carbohydrate: 34 g
protein: 8 g

3 Return the cream mixture to the stove and bring to the scald again (do not boil). Add half of the cream mixture to the egg mixture while whisking to combine. Add the newly combined mixture to the remaining cream mixture in the saucepan and stir to combine and thicken slightly.

4 Remove the pan from the heat and place into a large bowl of iced water to cool rapidly.

5 Fill individual ramekins with mixture, place in a deep baking dish and place into the oven. Add enough water to the dish to come halfway up the sides of the ramekins. Cover with a sheet of greaseproof paper and cook until set: approximately 30–40 minutes.

6 Cool to room temperature and then refrigerate. When cool, top with caster sugar and burn with a cooking blowtorch torch or under a grill until caramelised.

# ricotta fritters with orange sauce

### ingredients

*sauce*
1 cup orange juice, strained
⅓ cup caster sugar
2 tablespoons butter
40 ml cream
1 tablespoon triple sec or cointreau

*fritters*
1 cup oil, for frying
250 g fresh ricotta, mashed
¼ cup plain flour, sifted
2½ tablespoons caster sugar
2 eggs
1 tablespoon orange zest
2 tablespoons icing sugar
1 orange, segmented

**serves 4**

**i**

**preparation time**
10 minutes

**cooking time**
15 minutes

**nutritional value**
fat: 51 g
carbohydrate: 51 g
protein: 12.5 g

1 In a small saucepan, combine the orange juice, sugar, butter, cream and triple sec. Heat until butter has melted, and bring to the boil. Reduce the heat and simmer until the sauce thickens.

2 Heat the oil in a large frying pan. Place all ingredients for fritters in a large bowl and mix together until well combined.

3 Place 1 tablespoon of mixture in the hot oil to make each fritter. Cook 3–4 at a time for 1–2 minutes each, turning over to cook on both sides. Take out with a slotted spoon and drain on paper towel.

4 To serve the fritters, pour over the orange sauce, dust with icing sugar and garnish with orange segments.

# individual fig puddings

## ingredients

250 g dried figs, chopped
1 cup water
1 teaspoon bicarbonate of soda
2 eggs
60 g butter
¾ cup caster sugar
1 cup self-raising flour
1 vanilla bean
1 teaspoon vanilla extract
**butterscotch sauce**
1 cup brown sugar
20 ml cream
30 g unsalted butter
**serves 4**

**i**

**preparation time**
5 minutes

**cooking time**
30 minutes

**nutritional value**
fat: 16.5 g
carbohydrate: 93 g
protein: 6.5 g

1 Preheat the oven to 190°C. Place the figs, water and bicarbonate of soda in a saucepan and cook for about 20 minutes, or until mixture has reached a jam consistency.

2 Pour the fig mixture into a bowl and beat in the remaining ingredients. Split the vanilla bean down the middle, scrape out the seeds and add them to the mixture.

3 Pour the mixture into individual ramekins or timbale-moulds and bake for 25 minutes.

4 To make the butterscotch sauce, combine all the ingredients in a saucepan, and stir over a low heat until sugar dissolves.

5 Serve the individual puddings with the sauce and cream or ice-cream.

# hazelnut brownies

## ingredients

½ cup unsweetened chocolate pieces
1 cup plain flour
2 teaspoons cocoa
½ teaspoon baking powder
½ teaspoon salt
90 g butter
150 ml extra virgin olive oil
1 tablespoon vanilla extract
2 cups sugar
4 eggs
1½ cup hazelnuts, coarsely chopped
**makes approximately 2 dozen**

**1** Preheat the oven to 180°C. Line a 20 cm square baking dish with greaseproof paper. Melt the chocolate slowly in 30-second intervals in the microwave on a medium heat.

**2** Sift together the flour, cocoa, baking powder and salt into a separate bowl and set aside.

**3** Melt the butter and beat with the olive oil, vanilla and sugar in a large bowl until combined. Add the eggs one at a time, then stir in the melted chocolate.

**4** Gently stir in all dry ingredients, being careful not to over-mix. Add one cup of nuts.

**5** Pour the mixture into the greased and lined baking tin and sprinkle over the remaining nuts. Bake for 25–30 minutes, until the brownies begin to pull away from the sides of the pan. Test with a skewer: they should still be soft but not raw-looking.

**6** Cool in the baking tray on a wire rack and then refrigerate before cutting into squares.

i

**preparation time**
8 minutes

**cooking time**
30 minutes

**nutritional value**
fat: 15 g
carbohydrate: 23 g
protein: 3 g

# glossary

**al dente:** Italian term to describe pasta and rice that is cooked until tender but still firm to the bite.

**bake blind:** to bake pastry cases without their fillings. Line the raw pastry case with greaseproof paper and fill with raw rice or dried beans. Remove paper and fill 5 minutes before completion of cooking time.

**baste:** to spoon hot cooking liquid over food at intervals during cooking to moisten and flavour it.

**beat:** to make a mixture smooth with rapid and regular motions using a spatula, wire whisk or electric mixer; to make a mixture light and smooth by enclosing air.

**beurre manié:** equal quantities of butter and flour mixed together to a smooth paste and stirred bit by bit into a soup, stew or sauce while on the heat to thicken. Stop adding when desired thickness results.

**bind:** to add egg or a thick sauce to hold ingredients together when cooked.

**blanch:** to plunge some foods into boiling water for less than a minute and then immediately plunge into iced water. This is to brighten the colour of some vegetables; and to remove skin from tomatoes and nuts.

**blend:** to mix 2 or more ingredients thoroughly together; do not confuse with blending in an electric blender.

**boil:** to cook in a liquid brought to boiling point and kept there.

**boiling point:** when bubbles rise continually and break over the entire surface of the liquid, reaching a temperature of 100ºC (212ºF). In some cases food is held at this high temperature for a few seconds then heat is turned to low for slower cooking. See **simmer**.

**bouquet garni:** a bundle of several herbs tied together with string for easy removal, placed into pots of stock, soups and stews for flavour. A few sprigs of fresh thyme, parsley and bay leaf are used; can be purchased in sachet form for convenience.

**caramelise:** to heat sugar in a heavy-based pan until it liquefies and develops a caramel colour. Vegetables such as blanched carrots and fried onions may be sprinkled with sugar and caramelised.

**chill:** to place in the refrigerator or stir over ice until cold.

**clarify:** to make a liquid clear by removing sediments and impurities. To melt fat and remove any sediment.

**coat:** to dust or roll food items in flour to cover the surface before the food is cooked. Also, to coat in flour, then egg and breadcrumbs.

**cool:** to stand at room temperature until some or all heat is removed, e.g. cool a little, cool completely.

**cream:** to make a mixture creamy and fluffy by working it with the back of a wooden spoon. Usually refers to creaming butter and sugar or margarine. May also be done with an electric mixer.

**croutons:** small cubes of bread, toasted or fried, used as an addition to salads or as a garnish to soups and stews.

**crudités:** raw vegetable sticks served with a dipping sauce.

**crumb:** to coat foods in flour, egg and breadcrumbs before frying. Adds flavour and texture and enhances appearance.

**cube:** to cut into small pieces with six even sides, e.g. cubes of meat.

**cut in:** to combine fat and flour using 2 knives scissor fashion or with a pastry blender, to make pastry.

**deglaze:** to dissolve dried-out cooking juices left on the base and sides of a roasting dish or frying pan. Add a little water, wine or stock, scrape and stir over heat until dissolved. The resulting liquid is used to make a flavoursome gravy or added to a sauce or casserole.

**degrease:** to skim fat from the surface of cooking liquids, e.g. stocks, soups, casseroles.

**dice:** to cut into small cubes.

**dredge:** to heavily coat with icing sugar, sugar, flour or cornflour.

**dressing:** a mixture added to completed dishes to add moisture and flavour, e.g. salads, cooked vegetables.

**drizzle:** to pour in a fine thread-like stream moving over a surface.

**egg wash:** beaten egg with milk or water used to brush pastry, bread dough or biscuits to give a sheen and golden brown colour.

**essence:** a strong flavouring liquid, usually made by distillation. Only a few drops are needed to flavour.

**fillet:** a piece of prime meat, fish or poultry which is boneless or has all bones removed.

**flake:** to separate cooked fish into flakes, removing any bones and skin, using a fork.

**flame:** to ignite warmed alcohol over food or to pour into a pan with food, ignite, then serve.

**flute:** to make decorative indentations around a pastry rim before baking.

**fold in:** combining a light, whisked or creamed mixture with other ingredients. Add a portion of the other ingredients at a time and mix using a gentle circular motion, over and under the mixture so that air will not be lost. Use a silver spoon or spatula.

**glaze:** to brush or coat food with a liquid that will give the finished product a glossy appearance, and on baked products, a golden brown colour.

**grease:** to rub the surface of a dish with oil or fat, to prevent food from sticking.

**herbed butter:** softened butter mixed with finely chopped fresh herbs and re-chilled. Serve with grilled meats and fish.

**hors d'oeuvres:** small savoury foods served as appetisers, popularly known today as 'finger food'.

**infuse:** to steep foods in a liquid until the liquid absorbs their flavour.

**joint:** to cut poultry and game into serving pieces by dividing at the joint.

**julienne:** to cut some food, (e.g. vegetables and processed meats) into fine strips the length of matchsticks. Used in salads or as a garnish to cooked dishes.

**knead:** to work a yeast dough in a pressing, stretching and folding motion with the heel of the hand until smooth and elastic to develop the gluten strands. Non-yeast doughs should be lightly and quickly handled, as gluten development is not desired.

**line:** to cover the inside of a baking tin with paper for the easy removal of the cooked product later.

**macerate:** to stand fruit in a syrup, liqueur or spirit to give it added flavour.

**marinade:** a flavoured liquid, into which food is placed for some time to give it flavour and to tenderise it. Marinades include an acid ingredient such as vinegar or wine, oil and seasonings.

**mask:** to evenly cover cooked food portions with a sauce, mayonnaise or savoury jelly.

**pan-fry:** to fry foods in a small amount of fat or oil, sufficient to coat the base of the pan.

**parboil:** to boil until partially cooked. The food is then finished by some other method.

**pare:** to peel the skin from vegetables and fruit. 'Peel' is the popular term but 'pare' is the name given to the knife used; a paring knife.

**pit:** to remove stones or seeds from olives, cherries, dates and so on.

**pith:** the white lining between the rind and flesh of citrus fruit.

**pitted:** fruit with the stone removed, e.g. pitted dates.

**poach:** to simmer gently in enough hot liquid to almost cover the food, so its shape will be retained.

**pound:** to flatten meat with a meat mallet or to reduce sonething to a paste or small particles with a mortar and pestle.

**simmer:** to cook in liquid just below boiling point at about 96°C (205°F) with small bubbles rising gently to the surface.

**skim:** to remove fat or froth from the surface of food.

**stock:** the liquid produced when meat, poultry, fish or vegetables have been simmered in water to extract the flavour. Used as a base for soups, sauces, casseroles etc. Convenience stock products are available.

**sweat:** to cook sliced onions or vegetables, in a small amount of butter in a covered pan over low heat, to soften them and release flavour without colouring.

# conversions

measurements differ from country to country and it's important to understand what the differences are. This guide gives you simple, 'at-a-glance' information for using the recipes in this book, wherever you may be. Cooking is not an exact science – minor variations in measurements won't make a great difference to the end result.

## equipment
The size of measuring spoons and cups used internationally differs slightly by about 2–3 teaspoons. We use the Australian standard metric measurements in our recipes:

**1 teaspoon = 5 ml**     **1 tablespoon = 20 ml**

**¹/₂ cup = 125 ml**     **1 cup = 250 ml**

**4 cups = 1 litre**

Measuring cups come in sets of one cup (250 ml), ¹/₂ cup (125 ml), ¹/₃ cup (80 ml) and ¹/₄ cup (60 ml). Use these for measuring liquids and certain dry ingredients.

Measuring spoons come in a set of four and should be used for measuring dry and liquid ingredients and guide.

When using cup or spoon measures always make them level, unless the recipe indicates otherwise.

## dry versus wet ingredients
While this system of measures is consistent for liquids, it's more difficult to quantify dry ingredients. For instance, one level cup equals, 200 g of brown sugar; 210 g of caster sugar; and 110 g of icing sugar.

When measuring dry ingredients such as flour, don't push the flour down or shake it into the cup. It is best just to spoon the flour in until it reaches the desired amount. When measuring liquids, use a clear vessel indicating metric levels.

Always use medium eggs (55–60 g) when eggs are required in a recipe.

## dry

| metric (grams) | imperial (ounces) |
|---|---|
| 30 g | 1 oz |
| 60 g | 2 oz |
| 90 g | 3 oz |
| 100 g | 3¹/₂ oz |
| 125 g | 4 oz |
| 150 g | 5 oz |
| 185 g | 6 oz |
| 200 g | 7 oz |
| 250 g | 8 oz |
| 280 g | 9 oz |
| 315 g | 10 oz |
| 330 g | 11 oz |
| 370 g | 12 oz |
| 400 g | 13 oz |
| 440 g | 14 oz |
| 470 g | 15 oz |
| 500 g | 16 oz (1 lb) |
| 750 g | 24 oz (1¹/₂ lb) |
| 1000 g (1 kg) | 32 oz (2 lb) |

## liquids

| metric (millilitres) | imperial (fluid ounces) |
|---|---|
| 30 ml | 1 fl oz |
| 60 ml | 2 fl oz |
| 90 ml | 3 fl oz |
| 100 ml | 3¹/₂ fl oz |
| 125 ml | 4 fl oz |
| 150 ml | 5 fl oz |
| 190 ml | 6 fl oz |
| 250 ml | 8 fl oz |
| 300 ml | 10 fl oz |
| 500 ml | 16 fl oz |
| 600 ml | 20 fl oz  (1 pint)* |
| 1000 ml (1 litre) | 32 fl oz |

*Note: an American pint is 16 fl oz.

### oven
Your oven should always be at the right temperature before placing the food in it to be cooked. Note that if your oven doesn't have a fan you may need to cook food for a little longer.

### microwave
It's difficult to give an exact cooking time for microwave cooking. It's best to watch what you are cooking closely to monitor its progress.

### standing time
Many foods continue to cook when you take them out of the oven or microwave. If a recipe states that the food needs to 'stand' after cooking, be sure not to overcook the dish.

### can sizes
The can sizes available in your supermarket or grocery store may not be the same as specified in the recipe. Don't worry if there is a small variation in size – it's unlikely to make a difference to the end result.

| cooking temperatures | °C (celsius) | °F (fahrenheit) | gas mark |
|---|---|---|---|
| very slow | 120 | 250 | 1/2 |
| slow | 150 | 300 | 2 |
| moderately slow | 160 | 315 | 2-3 |
| moderate | 180 | 350 | 4 |
| moderately hot | 190 | 375 | 5 |
|  | 200 | 400 | 6 |
| hot | 220 | 425 | 7 |
| very hot | 230 | 450 | 8 |
|  | 240 | 475 | 9 |
|  | 250 | 500 | 10 |

# index